Early Country Music

An eye witness account

Jan Edwards

ISBN 0-9720484-3-X

Distributed by:
¥ Jan Edwards
   11721 Parliament #301
   San Antonio, TX 78213
   210-525-1021
¥ MK Publishing
   St. Cloud, MN 56304
   800-551-1023

Published by:
¥ Mk Publishing
   www.yourbookpublisher.net

A good song reflects the true feelings of the heart. A personal photo tells the story.

- Jan Edwards

DEDICATION

This book is lovingly dedicated to Eddy Arnold, Ray Price and Jimmy Dean, my three heroes in early country music.

To my daughters, Terrie and Angie, who are also country music entertainers and to Wayne Clanton, who recalls the wonderful performers and their down to earth ballads of long ago.

To my dear Robin who always supports my endeavors through his love and protection.

My sincere gratitude to every country music star who has shared his or her life through song.

TABLE OF CONTENTS

A MUSICAL MIRACLE

EDDY ARNOLD PAVED THE WAY

SUNSHINE SUE S BARN DANCE

MY ASSOCIATION WITH THE BARN DANCE MEETING

THE GRAND OLE OPRY STARS

JIMMY DEAN   I.O.U. A MILLION THANKS

DANCING WITH KING ELVIS

JANIS MARTIN - THE FEMALE ELVIS

MRS. JIMMIE RODGERS

VISITING WITH A VARIETY OF STARS

Jan at age 4

A MUSICAL MIRACLE

My country tis of thee, Sweet land of liberty, Of thee
I sing. At age four, my tiny little fingers played the
notes of this song on my Aunt Belle s old upright piano.
I call it a musical miracle. I learned this song in
Sunday school and I didn t then nor have I ever taken
piano lessons. I was blessed with a divine gift of which I
am very grateful.

Being an only child born in Petersburg, Virginia to
Aubrey and Virginia Brough I often remember my mother
saying that I hummed songs before I walked or talked.

My dad never stopped believing that I d be involved
in the arts and entertainment field. If I heard a song
and liked the melody I would go very often to my aunt s
house and play it on the piano using one finger at a
time. By the time I started to school I had improved my
playing and my love for music was growing rapidly.

Mother was a devoted Baptist and was the choir
director at her church. She had a beautiful soprano
voice and loved to sing. Dad was a Presbyterian and led
the singing at his church. He also played the harmonica
at home in his spare time. I can still hear him playing
 The Wreck Of The Old 97 and Red Wing.

My mother s mother, the only grandmother I ever
knew, lived with us and was an avid fan of what then
was called hillbilly music.

Grandmother Hawkins spoke often of her brother
Stanley, who made all kinds of musical instruments out
of wood, tin, bottles and spoons and would get friends
together and they d play on the street corners every

Saturday night. They always sung the old cowboy songs and folk ballads

Mother and dad shared a great love for this type of music, especially the songs sung by Jimmie Davis and Red Foley.

When I was in the third grade, I played everything from Beautiful Dreamer to On Top Of Old Smokey. for my music class. It was the one class I looked forward to more than any other and I remember my teacher being in awe of my ability to play so many different songs without ever taking a lesson.

My little heart yearned desperately for a big piano of my own. It was out of the question though, because mother and daddy worked very hard at an Optical plant and their take home pay at that time was around twenty-nine dollars a week. There was never very much money left over, so only things of great necessity were bought. So this prompted me to go any place that had a piano so I could play.

I remember when I was eight years old, at Christmas that year, Santa Claus brought me a toy baby grand. It had all the features of a real baby grand and I was so proud of it. I pounded out songs on that little piano till my fingers were sore. Every song that I heard on the radio that I liked I d remember the melody and play it. My parents promised me that one day I d have a real piano whenever they could afford it.

I built my hopes on that promise and continued enjoying the little toy baby grand which was soon to play an important part in my love for country music.

EDDY ARNOLD PAVED THE WAY

Grandmother was a faithful listener to the Grand Ole Opry every Saturday evening. She considered it as much a proper thing to do as attending church on Sunday.

While she and I sat around the old Philco radio listening to the Opry she reminded me at my early age that this would always be good, clean entertainment coming from people who would share their everyday experiences in the form of song. She also said that as long as the world stood and the name Roy Acuff was held in memory, there would always be a Grand Ole Opry and that nothing would ever take its place.

One Saturday while we were listening, I heard a man with a soft, silkened voice sing a song called Many Tears Ago. I put my ear right up to the radio speaker so I wouldn t miss a sound. It was the prettiest voice I d ever heard. Yes indeed! It was the Tennessee Plowboy, Eddy Arnold.

It didn t take me long to go to the kitchen where mother was baking a cake for Sunday dinner to ask her if she would buy me a record by Eddy Arnold. I gave her the name of the song and she said that she would go to the music store the following Monday when she finished work and see if they had it. We had some old 78 RPM records, but not any by Eddy Arnold and we had an old cabinet style wind-up Victrola.

I remember one record Grandmother had was Pins and Needles by Roy Acuff. She also had several by Ernest Tubb. She especially liked his record of Blue-eyed Elaine.

Monday finally rolled around and mother came home that evening with my Eddy Arnold record of Many

Tears Ago. I jumped for joy and immediately went to the Victrola and played it over and over about twenty times until I learned the tune. Then I started playing it on my little toy baby grand. A few days later I learned the flip side, which was Mommy Please Stay Home With Me. Mother started buying all of Eddy s records for me as soon as they were in the store.

With the help of my grandmother, I started writing a letter once a week to my Hero, who was also appearing on THE EDDY ARNOLD SHOW, which was on each Saturday morning on a local station in my home town and was sponsored by The Purina Company. He often acknowledged me by singing If You ll Let Me Be Your Little Sweetheart and he sent me a postcard photo of him that included his autograph.

I collected all of his records and songbooks and eventually learned to play all of his songs on my toy piano. When friends or relatives would visit us on Sunday, they would always ask me to play for them.

I was so infatuated with Eddy s voice that I spent my spare time everyday listening to his records while other kids were outside playing. I made it a point to learn all the old songs like, Be Sure There s No Mistake,   I Talk To Myself About You and Chained To A Memory, which would grow to be my all time favorite song by Eddy.

This was the beginning of my love for hillbilly music and every Saturday would find me sitting with my grandmother waiting for Eddy s show in the morning and the Grand Ole Opry in the evening.

I remember Ernest Tubb starting off his portion of the show with his famous Walking The Floor Over You. I thought one of the saddest songs he sang was The Soldier s Last Letter.

Roy Acuff did his famous Wabash Cannonball and The Great Speckled Bird. My favorite by him was We Live In Two Different Worlds.

Cowboy Copas would come on singing, Signed, Sealed and Delivered and Moon Mullican would sing I ll Sail My Ship Alone while playing the piano. I admired Moon s playing a lot and I wrote him that I also played and he sent me an autographed picture and wrote on a little card and wished me luck in my music.

It was such fun to hear Minnie Pearl exclaim, Howdee! I m just so proud to be here.

I was falling in love with all of these people and found myself begging my parents and my grandmother to buy me records by them. Back then, they were all recording on 78 RPM records and you could purchase them real cheap. I still have some of those old records and I ve put them all on tape in case they get broken.

On Sunday mornings, early before we would leave for church, we always listened to the Renfro Valley Hour, a program that originated from Renfro Valley, Kentucky. They sang all the old time hymns and I had a friend on the show that I admired. His name was Clay Eager.

When I was twelve years old, my parents bought an old Henry F. Miller upright piano for me. I ll never forget the day I came home from school and saw my piano sitting in the living room.Grandmother was sitting in her rocking chair waiting to see the look on my face and she said, Now you can play all those Eddy Arnold songs you love so well. I was so overwhelmed with joy, I started playing every song I knew, over and over again.

By the time I was fourteen, my best girlfriend and I were singing on a local radio station. We called ourselves The Cowgirl Sweethearts. My parents had bought me a piano accordion for my birthday and I played it on the show. My friend played guitar and we had two guys that sang with us. I had developed a strong sense for yodeling and loved to do a song called Cowboy s Sweetheart. Patsy Montana had a big hit with this song and so did Rosalie Allen.

Some friends of the family had also blessed me with a banjo and a steel guitar, so I was well on my way to playing the sounds of country music on various instruments. I was well aware that this kind of entertainment was definitely going to be a big part of my life and that sometime in the near future, I would be mingling with the stars.

My first meeting with
Eddy Arnold

Eddy signing
my book

Grandma & Jan

Jan

Jan

Jan

Sunshine Sue in early years

SUNSHINE SUE S BARN DANCE

In 1946, another show began its history in
Richmond, Virginia. Organized and directed by Mary
Arlene Workman, better known as Sunshine Sue, the
Old Dominion Barn Dance, was held each Saturday at
the WRVA Theater, at 9th and Broad Streets.

Remembering the many on-stage introductions for its
beautiful and gracious femcee hostess, I can still hear
Al Aaroe, Ray Kennedy and Carl Stutz saying Here s
the pretty dark-eyed sweetheart, smooth talking, sweet
singing, Sunshine Sue and she d immediately make
her entrance singing her rendition of You Are My
Sunshine, which became her famous theme song.

Her stage name was given to her years before by a
fellow radio station worker who said that anyone who
looked that beautiful and had that big smile all the
while should be called Sunshine, so the name
Sunshine Sue was given to Mrs. Workman.

Sue was originally from Keosauqua, Iowa and she
married her childhood sweetheart, John Workman and
their singing careers led them to the National Barn
Dance in Chicago and on to Richmond in the 1940 s.

Sue and her Rangers, John and Sam Workman, had
a radio show on WRVA several years prior to her
starting the Barn Dance. Her love for good old hillbilly
music and performers like Jimmie Davis, Red Foley and
Gene Autry, inspired her to put together a family show
for people to attend. She also took the show on the road
to all parts of Virginia, playing in many high schools.

The Barn Dance was broadcast daily, morning and mid-afternoon, which left barely enough time for them to leave after the show to drive to their personal appearances.

Every time they would come to my high school, I was there waiting, long before they d arrive. My girlfriend and I would wait after school with a packed lunch on the front steps, usually about three hours until some of the cast would start driving up and then we would meet some of them and go in with them. This started my close friendship with all of the people on the show and my great admiration for Sunshine Sue, who I thought was the most beautiful lady I had ever seen.

She wore a big smile constantly and the whole room just seemed to light up when you were in her presence. She wore lovely cotton dresses that I found out later were all made by her and she always wore flowers in her hair to match her dresses. I also remember how she loved her golden locket, which she wore on a black velvet band around her neck. Her steep high heeled shoes always matched the color of her dress.

My camera at that time took only black and white pictures and I took dozens of photos, so that started my collection of all the entertainers.

I hurried home from school each day just in time to listen to the afternoon Barn Dance with my grandmother. I was in my first year of high school now and my life was becoming more and more involved with these wonderful singers and shows.

One day I was looking through our local paper and I noticed an advertisement about Eddy Arnold coming to Richmond, which was about 30 miles from our city. When my parents came home from work that evening, I begged them to send for tickets. To do something like this was a real luxury in those days and even more so since we had to travel by bus to get there. My dad thought it over and said he would go and borrow the money from a local finance company and we d go to see Eddy s show in the afternoon and to the Barn Dance in the evening. I can t tell you how happy I was and I could hardly wait for the day to arrive.

Sue & Jan
before showtime

Sunshine Sue at Petersburg
High School

Sue placing her
matching flower
in her hair

Sunshine Sue

June Carter

Sue & John Workman

The Carter Family

Mother Maybelle & daughter Helen

Grandpa Jones & Ramona

Grandpa Jones & Ramona

Joe Maphis
playing the
Orange
Blossom Special

Joe Maphis

The Show finally came and it was a day in my life that I ll never forget. Eddy sang all of his hits and the highlight came when I got to meet him after the show and take pictures. He was so kind and thanked me over and over for writing to him so often and told my parents how glad he was that they brought me to see his show. Believe me, those were the happiest moments of my life.

We had a couple of hours to eat supper and then go to the Barn Dance. I could hardly eat for rehearsing the whole Eddy Arnold show. We were in a small restaurant called The White Tower which was across the street from the WRVA Theater where we would be attending the Barn Dance.

I looked outside the window and saw some of the cast, including June Carter and John Workman, so we went out to see them and they remembered me, of course, from being at the high school at home. We took some pictures and John invited us to go backstage with them to see Sue. I must have taken 24 pictures while we were back there talking and I told Sue that I wanted to start a fan club for her and the Barn Dance. She was so pleased and said she would help me any way she could and she could supply me with large photos of the cast.

Before we knew it, the first show was about to get under way, so we hurried to claim our reserved seats which were on the front row, It was so wonderful to see Sunshine Sue come on stage singing You Are My Sunshine. Jimmie Davis wrote that song, but it was definitely meant for Sue to sing it and it became her trademark.

Later in the show, Sue sang a couple of songs that were traditional. One was Red River Valley and the other was My Mother s Old Sunbonnet. Sue most always played her piano accordion while singing. She also played the piano, bass and ukulele. Her Rangers often sang chorus background.

When it was time for the Carter Family to sing they brought Mother Maybelle to the microphone to do her famous Wildwood Flower. The family followed up with

Green Grow The Lilacs. June was the comedian and she sang a novelty song called Keep Them Cold Icy Fingers Off Of Me. Anita gave her best at yodeling and had many requests for Swiss Yodel and Freight Train Blues. Helen played accordion and sang along with the group and sometimes sang solos.

Grandpa Jones and his wife Ramona were favorites. He was a man in his thirties, but portrayed the image of Grandpa. He strummed a mean banjo and sang about Old Rattler. Ramona was a champion fiddler player and pleased her audience with Orange Blossom Special.

Bonnie, Bea and Buster, The Puffenbarger Kids, were an excellent trio and Buster was an extraordinary accordionist.

Joe Maphis was a master musician. He had been with the Barn Dance from its beginning. He played every instrument known to mankind and sang such songs as Philadelphia Lawyer and I m My Own Grandpa.

Rose and Mary, the Saddle Sweethearts, were two lovely ladies from Maryland who had been singing together for several years. They wore cowgirl suits and boots and were famous for their song, When I Yoo Hoo In The Valley.

The show featured numerous entertainers from the east coast, like Charlie Bailey, Curley Howard, the Tobacco Tags, Bill and Benny Kissinger and Curley Collins.

As time went on, the Fan Club I d organized grew immensely. It didn t take long to reach the 3,000 mark because the listening audience was vast, as well as the attendance at the Theater on Saturday nights.

Sue & Rangers - Joe, John & Sam

Sunshine Sue & Joe Maphis

Rose & Mary - The Saddle Sweethearts

Sunshine Sue & Jan

MY ASSOCIATION WITH THE BARN DANCE

After my high school days were over, I decided I wanted to be more closely associated with Sunshine Sue and the Barn Dance. I worked with for a local music store during the week and every weekend I traveled by bus to Richmond. I would leave very early in the morning and sometimes I would spend the day with Sue and sometimes with my friends, Rose and Mary, the Saddle Sweethearts.

Sue had an office at the Hotel Richmond, across the hall from the WRVA studios, where I spent many hours doing fan club work: preparing newsletters and journals and answering mail for Sue and constantly signing up new members.

Sometimes I would sit at the reception desk by the switchboard late on Saturday nights after the last show to meet and talk with people who were staying in the hotel that had attended the show.

My front row seats at the Barn Dance were reserved every week and Sue always dedicated one of her songs to me and our club. Two of my favorites were, Smiles Are Made Of Sunshine and Say Something Good About Someone.

One Saturday in 1952, we had Fan Club night on the show. Our members all went together and got so many nice things for Sue including some crystal and a pair of lamps, a beautifully decorated tier cake and corsage. They were all displayed on a long table and rolled out on stage, much to her surprise. It was my

pleasure to introduce this lovely lady of song and my
club vice president and I sang You Are My Sunshine
with her. It was a memorable event and one that Sue
and the cast appreciated so much.

From time to time, new artists would join the Barn
Dance to keep the show fresh with new talent. Sue
planned her own programs and hired the talent she
thought best to please her audience. Thousands came
from all over the country to view the show and
countless others listened to it on the air waves and on
the CBS Radio Network.

Sunshine Sue became so popular that she was
crowned Queen Of The Hillbillies by William M. Tuck,
who was once Governor of Virginia. Dwight and Mamie
Eisenhower were both fans of the show and were
honorable members of our club.

As time went on, many performers joined the Barn
Dance and gained popularity before going on to the
Grand Ole Opry. Stars like Lester Flatt and Earl
Scruggs, Chet Atkins, Wilma Lee and Stoney Cooper
and Mac Wiseman.

Hawkshaw Hawkins and Jean Shepard, Martha
Carson and Bill Carlisle were often guests on the show.

Abbie Neal and her Ranch Girls made a lasting
impression on the audience. Abbie not only played the
fiddle to perfection, she was one of the best steel
guitarists in the business.

Sue also had a talk show once a week, where she
invited many celebrities to join her. Even with this busy
schedule she always found time to maintain her home,
do he own cooking and care for her two children, Bill
and Virginia Sue.

New groups were still joining our show like Ralph
and Carter Stanley, Don Reno and Red Smiley and
their famous comedy skit called The One and Only
Tennessee Cut-Ups.

Besides singing such favorites as I m Using My Bible
For A Roadmap and I Know You re Married, But I
Love You Still, Reno and Smiley s portion of the show

presented good clean comedy, religious songs and instrumentals, as well. Reno was known as one of the country s greatest banjo players.

Another newcomer was Janis Martin, who was called The Female Elvis presley. She rocked the stage each Saturday and did all the moves just like Elvis and mastered all of his songs. She also wrote and recorded a big hit called, My Boy Elvis.

Slim Roberts, a smooth voiced balladeer, sang his version of I Wasted A Nickel Last Night.

Quincy Snodgrass kept the audience laughing with his jokes.What a show! and what top notch entertainment!

It was during my association with the Barn Dance that I had the opportunity to go to Washington D.C. when Sue would go there to do commercials. This enabled me to meet one of the finest people in the music industry, Jimmie Dean. He had a regular show on WTOP.

I also traveled to Wheeling West Virginia to attend the WWVA Wheeling Jamboree. Hawkshaw Hawkins, Toby Stroud, Wilma Lee and Stoney Cooper were all at one time members of the Jamboree.

My travels also took me to Mansfield, Ohio where I played briefly in Tex Foreman s Band which featured Reva, The Indian Girl.

Every day was country music day for me and to recall the memories brings back so much joy.

Lester Flatt and Earl Scruggs and the Foggy Mountain Boys were a big attraction on the Barn Dance.

I thought Lester had an unusual voice. I used to tell him that I could listen to him talk or sing for hours without a break. He used to say, How can you stand it? He always seemed to be totally relaxed both on and off stage.

Everyone knew that Earl Scruggs was a master musician. He could make his banjo talk with little or no effort. I still can hear the people in the audience yelling out, Play Flint Hill Special. He always had to play this song over a second time.

My favorite song by Flatt and Scruggs was I 11 Go
Stepping Too. Every time I d pass Lester in the hall at
the radio station, I d say don t forget my song and he d
smile and say Gotcha.

Sue, Jan & Nell - Fan Club Night

Mr. & Mrs. Red Foley

Randy Travis

Bill Carlisle & Band

Virginia Brough & Martha Carson
(Jan s mom)   (Gospel singer)

Martha Carson & Jan

Sunshine Sue
&
Dwight D.
Eisenhower

Sunshine Sue
& Gene Autry

Abbie Neal & The Ranch Girls

George Morgan
& Reva,
The Indian Girl

Sunshine Sue holding my daughter Terrie Sue, her beloved
namesake whom she adored

Earl Scruggs, Paul Warren, Curly Sechler & Lester Flatt

Lester Flatt & Earl Scruggs

Wilma Lee &
Stoney Cooper

Don Reno
& Red Smiley

Janis Martin, Zennie Cox
& Jan at WRVA

Slim Roberts

Slim and Ola Roberts

Fiddle Player Slim Roberts and Band

Slim Roberts and the Men of the West

Chet Atkins

Merle Travis

Buck Ryan

The Stanley Brothers

Whispering Bill Anderson & Jan

MEETING THE GRAND OLE OPRY STARS

I remember the first time I saw Marty Robbins. It was in the early 50 s and he was traveling on a show with Webb Pierce.

Both were riding high on the charts and Marty would drive the girls crazy when he d hit those high notes on Hawaiian songs. I sat next to one girl who got so excited that she fainted when he sang Aloha Oe.

Webb Pierce was tall and handsome and his smile charmed all the girls when he walked out on stage. We always said he was the best thing that ever came out of Sears and Roebuck, since he used to be a salesman for them. He had a remarkable sound in his voice, you could always understand every word. Songs like, How Do You Talk To A Baby and Back Street Affair were classics.

Marty had that mischievous smile and loved to clown around on stage. He had a distinctive sound, a voice that couldn t be copied. A White Sport Coat and A Pink Carnation became the trend for every high school Prom.

Traveling shows also brought Hawkshaw Hawkins to a local theater in my home town. He had two shows scheduled, one in the afternoon and another later in the evening. In between shows, we had dinner in a nearby restaurant. He was soft spoken and a very charming gentleman. His songs A Heartache To Recall and I Wasted A Nickel Last Night were on every juke box in the country, including the restaurant we were in.

Gene Autry was on tour across the country with his famous horse, Champion. He had a performance in Richmond and was a guest on Sunshine Sue s program.

My travels to Florida, brought lasting memories of the great Hank Williams. His unique style of writing and singing cheatin songs, always remained in our thoughts. You couldn t love country music and not love Hank Williams. He had an airy attitude, but he loved his fans and helped many people along the way.

I remember a statement that he made in my presence after a show one evening. He said, The only way we ll ever get by in this world is to help someone in some way, each day.

Wilma Lee and Stoney Cooper were two of the most down to earth people you d ever want to meet. Wilma Lee is an original mountain singer and she never strayed from old time country music nor from the inspirational ballads that she and Stoney sang like Thirty Pieces Of Silver and Tramp On The Street. They put a lasting mark on traditional gospel music. Their performances with the Clinch Mountain Clan, played to packed houses at the WWVA Wheeling, West Virginia Jamboree and the WRVA Barn Dance in Richmond, Virginia and later to the Grand Ole Opry in 1957.

Through it all, Buck Graves, a member of the Clan, played a very important part with his unique sound on the dobro steel guitar.

Wilma Lee proudly wore her pinafore dresses, made in colorful country patterns and always flashed a big smile as she approached the stage. Stoney dressed in his western business attire, wearing the perfect cowboy hat to match.

Every Ray Price fan at one time or another has wondered if his life has been as sad and heartbreaking as his songs portray. He s gifted with a voice that compares to no other performer and a style that s entirely his own. Every song he sings touches the heart of both young and old, describing the hurts, sorrows and disappointments that life has to offer. His career began in the fifties and when his song Crazy Arms topped the charts in 1956, he turned out one hit after the other from then on. His band, The Cherokee

Cowboys were a dominant part in his music. They had a sound that when heard, one immediately knew Ray Price was up front to sing. He was much inspired by Hank Williams and patterned a lot of his songs after his style.

Johnny Bush and Darrel McCall perform in certain fashions that remind you of the Ray Price sound. Each, a star in his own right, keep the people in San Antonio, Texas, happy with their music.

The first time I saw Johnny Cash was in Lawton, Oklahoma. He was on the same show with George Jones and Johnny Horton. I always thought his ballad of Lorena was an outstanding contribution to his collection of songs.

I was fortunate to meet Brenda Lee, in Washington, D.C. when she was just a little girl starting in the music business. She was tiny, but had a mighty voice. Now to hear her sing her rendition of Johnny Ray s hit called Cry, is to understand what a great talent she possesses.

Faron Young had one of the best voices in country music. Looking back to his performances on the Louisiana Hayride, Faron always had a big fan following. When he had his first hit, Goin Steady every girl in the nation within listening range of the record, wanted to go steady with him.

After spending time in the Army, he returned to the music industry and began turning hit after hit. If I had to choose a favorite, it would be Four In The Morning. We used to have a saying that you d have to go to bed at four in the morning and get up at one minute past four to get past that beautiful singing voice.

Faron was given the title, The Young Sheriff because of his role in the movie, Hidden Guns. He was known to be very outspoken and also for his great sense of humor.

Mac Wiseman, better known as The Voice With A Heart, has a reputation for knowing more old time songs than anyone in the business. Each song he sings is done with heart felt sincerity. When he was a member of the Barn Dance in Richmond, Virginia, he

brought unending applause when he sang Davy
Crockett and Love Letters In The Sand.
     Gentleman, Jim Reeves, had one of the smoothest
voices in country music. When he sang Danny Boy,
you could hear a pin drop. It touched everyone in the
audience, young and old. He had a fantastic band that
knew exactly how to bring his music alive. Dean
Manuel, Bobby Dyson and Leo Jackson played a big
part in his show.
     Porter Wagoner has to be one of the most dedicated
people in the country music era. He expresses his
sincere love for country music and its performers every
time you see him on the Opry. He always has a good
word for each musician and a hearty welcome and
makes them feel right at home. No one could have
deserved the title, Ambassador To Opryland more
than this friendly and outgoing gentleman. He ll always
be remembered for his hit record of Satisfied Mind
and for his beautiful rhinestone studded cowboy suits
made by Nudie Cohen.
     When the words country music come to mind, you
automatically think of George Jones. When asking
anyone about the all time favorite country song, it has
to be He Stopped Loving Her Today. George s life
experiences through songs puts him at the top of the
performer s list.
     Countless female singers have made their mark in
the field. Kitty Wells started a whole new outlook with I
Didn t Know God Made Honky Tonk Angels and
Tammy Wynette taught us all to Stand By Your Man.
     Connie Smith gave her best at Once A Day while
Jeannie Pruett blessed the economy with the sale of
Satin Sheets.
     Skeeter Davis tells us I ve Forgot More Than You ll
Ever Know and Dolly Parton wore a Coat Of Many
Colors. Patsy Cline took us Walkin After Midnight
and Dottie West raised us on Country Sunshine.
     Remember the good old duets like Bill Anderson and
Jan Howard singing For Loving You and Dolly and
Porter singing Just Someone I Used To Know. Jim Ed

Brown and Helen Cornelius, Kitty Wells and Red Foley and Loretta and Conway all sang beautiful duets. Those were the good old days.

Little Jimmy Dickens is a real showman. I 11 never forget the first time I saw his show in Virginia. He was wearing a bright yellow western suit and he came out on stage bouncing from one end to the other and I thought he was the cutest thing I ever saw. This was back in the early 50 s. I couldn t believe how much he jumped up and down while he sang. It wore me out just watching him and I called him a little bit of dynamite energy from then on. He was so nice to talk with and just smiled the whole time we talked. Aside from his trademark songs like Take An Old Cold Tater and Wait he could sing a beautiful ballad which was my all time favorite by him called We Could.

Ira and Charlie Louvin gave us many heartfelt songs that will always be remembered. One of their most popular was When I Stop Dreaming and was certainly my favorite. They dressed alike on stage and their voices blended in perfect harmony. I remember my first talk with them in 1956, they were both so friendly and I called Charlie Little Charlie from then on.

Buck or Josh Graves has played with the best of them. He went by both names at separate times. I knew him as Buck when he was a part of the Clinch Mountain Clan with Wilma Lee and Stoney Cooper. He could really play the dobro and was known for his mischievous smile all the while.

Don Helms had a sound on the steel guitar that no one else could attempt to match. It was this sound that made Hank Williams music recognizable immediately. A likeable fellow, Don has always had time to talk with country music fans, even to this day as he travels sometimes across country. I liked his broad smile and he was easy to talk to about the music business.

Carl Smith and June Carter were married for a short time, they had a daughter, Carlene who is also in show business, a star in her own right.

A great brother duet team were the Wilburn
Brothers. They toured a lot with Webb Pierce and also
Faron Young. When I first met them back in the early
50 s I couldn t tell them apart for the longest time.
Their stage performances were fantastic, they always
dressed alike in western attire and they would keep
changing places as they were performing to make the
crowds wonder which one was which. I always thought
one of their best songs was Troubles Back In Town.
Their voices blended so well together in ballads and
also in gospel songs.I used to kid Teddy back then, by
asking if they ever got into arguments and he replied,
 Who,us? Never I d look over at Doyle and he d be
winking his eye at that answer. It was the Wilburn
Brothers who introduced Loretta Lynn. She traveled
with them quite a bit early in her career.

I was so fortunate to meet Hank Sugarfoot Garland
back in the early 50 s in Washington, D.C. He was a
marvelous guitar player and his contributions were
on so many top artist records like Patsy Cline and
Don Gibson.

Hank had an automobile accident in the early 60 s
that left him unable to continue his career. I have quite
a few of the older records that he played on and I still
enjoy listening to his style for he could play any kind of
song: country, blues, jazz or pop.

George Morgan had that Eddy Arnold touch in his
voice. I met him in El Paso, Texas and he was the
perfect gentleman but he was a big tease and he liked
to pull pranks on fellow entertainers. George loved Coca
Cola. When I talked with him backstage I had my little
girl with me, whom he fell in love with and he said
 Wait just a minute and let me get my coke and we ll
take all the pictures you want.   I just loved to hear him
sing Cry Baby Heart and he dedicated it to me on his
show that night. He was nationally famous for his song
 Candy Kisses and I don t think I ve ever eaten a
chocolate kiss without reminders of this man.

Red Foley, who could ever mistake that smooth
voice? As a child I listened to Red on the Renfro Valley

Barn Dance and then I finally got to meet him in El Paso in 1963. What a wonderful person! So down to earth, so polite and kind and caring. He sat with my little girl on his lap talking to her for a long time.

One of my favorite songs by Red was a recording he did in the 40 s on Decca called A Pillow Of Sighs and Tears. He was known nationally for his gospel song Peace In The Valley.

It was Red Foley who inspired the big name change from hillbilly to country for America s traditional country music.

Marty Robbins

Marty Robbins

Marty Robins and Jerrie Steinhardt

Marty Robbins and Jim Steinhardt

Webb Pierce

Red Sovine & Webb Pierce

Webb Pierce

Jim Reeves

Don Helms

Carl Smith & June Carter

The Wilburn Brothers

Hawshaw Hawkins

Slim Whitman, Hank Snow & Mac Wiseman

Hank Williams

Hank Williams, Jr.

Hank Williams

Brenda Lee & little fan

Ray Price

Darrell McCall & Jan

Faron Young

Faron Young & Jan

Mac Wiseman & Terrie Edwards

Minnie Pearl & Roy Acuff

Jan & WIlma Lee

WIlma Lee & Stoney

Johnny Cash

Carl Smith & June carter

Aubrey Brough (Jan s Dad)
& Buddy Allen

Homer & Jethro

Carol Cooper

Little Jimmy Dickens
& Carl Smith

Porter & Sunshine Sue

JIMMY DEAN - I.O.U. A MILLION THANKS

Joe Maphis was a master musician. He was a
natural born guitarist from Suffolk, Virginia and had
decided when he was 17 years old to master the guitar.
Even though he had his own distinctive technique on
the guitar strings, many thought he was a reminiscent
of Merle Travis.

Joe covered the globe during his career. He joined
Sunshine Sue and her Rangers in 1938. A short time
thereafter, he moved on to the WLS National Barn
Dance in Chicago.

Soon, World War II found him in the Army s Special
Services entertaining the troops in the Pacific for 20
months. After the war, he decided to go back and join
Sunshine Sue s newly organized Barn Dance. It was
during this time that Joe met his wife to be, pretty little
Rose Lee, of the Saddle Sweethearts. They hit it off right
away and soon were married.

Joe played his favorite instrument, a double necked
guitar, of very high value. He also played ever other
instrument he could get his hands on. What a performer!
He could make the old time bass fiddle talk and he
mastered Orange Blossom Special on the fiddle,
playing it in every position: over the head, behind the
back, under the arm and leg and Lying down on the
floor with his feet up in the air. He played bluegrass
tunes on the mandolin and banjo and could play most
any song on the accordion and piano. He also
composed both music and Lyrics. Joe recorded Barn
Dance Boogie, a song he wrote and took turns playing
it on various instruments.

He often played the comedian role of Cousin Crazy
Joe dressed in a pair of trousers big enough for a team
of mules and frequently brought his old jalopy car
called Cindy on stage. He also played a guitar made
from a toilet seat. This kept the audience in stitches
throughout the show.

In the early 50 s Joe and Rose Lee moved to California
and joined Town Hall Party. While recording for Okey
Records they had two big hits, Dim Lights, Thick
Smoke and Loud Music and Black Mountain Rag.

Joe obtained a part in Universal Pictures, The Benny
Goodman Story with James Stewart, Dell Porter and
Skeets McDonald and as a team they sang Little
Brown Jug. Joe never took any credit for himself. He
was always praising fellow musician Merle Travis and
looked up to him as the best.

Willie Nelson has written and recorded some great songs.
He s been fortunate that so many artists have recorded
his songs and the awards have been unending. The first
time I met Willie was at the Big D Jamboree in Dallas,
Texas in the early sixties. He was with Shirley Collie.
He was a very soft spoken gentleman. Through the years
he has done so much to help the farmers of America.

When I met Jimmy Dean, he had a series of daily
and weekend shows that were produced by Connie B.
Gay in Washington, D.C. During our first conversation
after a television show, I realized immediately that he
was down to earth, sincere and warmhearted and a
person who really cared about his audience, their likes
and dislikes. Here was a man who wanted to be free to
be himself, to express his true feelings through song.
Jimmy Dean could never portray something or someone
whom he wasn t. When I told him how much I enjoyed
his show and his accordion playing he must have
thanked me a dozen times.

Jimmy gained fame in the nation s Capitol especially
on the Town and Country Jamboree. He was sent to
the Caribbean, Panama and to Europe to entertain the
servicemen. Several years later, he skyrocketed to the
top with a song he wrote on a plane trip from Dallas to

New York called Big Bad John. He never dreamed it
would be a smash hit.

Country music s best recitationist gifted his audience
with I.O.U., penned for his mother and To A Sleeping
Beauty, a tribute to his daughter, Connie. I have never
listened to these songs without tear-filled eyes and have
never heard Jimmy recite them without his own deep
emotion bursting forth. His heartfelt sentiments are
what earned him a reputation as a great recitationist.

There are thousands like me, that miss the kind of
entertainment that Jimmy had on his country-style
ABC Television Variety Show. He once signed a picture
for me that read, Thanks a million, Jan. Now it s my
turn to say, Jimmy Dean, I.O.U. a million thanks for
all the happiness you ve brought into my life through
your songs.

Aubrey Brough & Merle Travis

Nobuko, Merle Travis & Jan

Rose & Joe Maphis with Jan

Shirley Collie & Willie Nelson

Marvin Carroll & Jimmy Dean

Jimmy Dean, Buck Ryan, Marvin Carroll & Herbie Jones

DANCING WITH KING ELVIS

The late summer of 1955, brought me in contact with one of the world s greatest performers. The show was to originate at an open-air grandstand near the Naval Base in Norfolk, Virginia.

After the regular Saturday night Barn Dance, I caught a bus to Norfolk to prepare for the show that headlined Hank Snow and the Rainbow Ranch Boys, his son, Jimmie Rodgers Snow, plus the Davis Sisters, Slim Whitman and Onie Wheeler.

Also, at the bottom of the billing was a fellow we d never heard of by the name of Elvis Presley.

In all the hustle bustle that Sunday afternoon talking with Hank and his son and visiting with Skeeter Davis, I still didn t even get a glimpse of who Elvis Presley was.

The curtains opened and the show began in its line-up order. The crowd was huge and as was always customary, I had a reserved seat on the front row center.

Everyone was having a great time. Halfway through the show they called a short intermission and then went on to the second half. I could hear people all around me saying, Who in the world is this dude called Elvis Presley? They weren t even pronouncing his name right.

After all the performers had their turn and everything became as quiet as a mouse on Christmas Eve, Hank Snow went and stood alongside the stage to watch. A local disc jockey came out and said everyone should make welcome this new star. Then the music started playing and out came a guy who brought a whole new era to American music. Holding his guitar, chewing gum a mile a minute and taking his comb from his coat pocket and combing his hair back with a teased look upon his face, he started belting out a song called That s All Right Mama. The crowd went wild. It was almost unbelievable. The puzzled looks on everyone s faces left. They knew at that moment without a doubt, who the singing rage Elvis Presley was!

He was scheduled to do only two songs, the previous one and Baby Let s Play House. The audience couldn t get enough, they screamed and screamed for more. Elvis came back out with that teased look and crooked smile and said. Thank you, Thank you very much, I was coming back anyway! The crowds reaction was overwhelming. The show finally came to an end with all of the entertainers standing on each end of the stage watching this young man who was to become a legend in his time.

After the show, I immediately went to talk to Elvis and found him to be the most polite and kind person I d ever met. He seemed very bashful and shocked that I should like his style of singing so much. He even commented that he didn t think he could sing that well at all but he sure loved trying and that his main ambition in life was to see that his folks had every thing that they needed. He talked so much about his love for his parents.

We chatted quite some time and he made me promise to meet him the next day in Richmond where the group would be performing for an evening show. He asked me to be there early because they would arrive shortly after noon. I agreed!

Coming back from Norfolk that night, I couldn t get Elvis off my mind. I was very anxious to meet him that next day. I definitely wanted to be on time, so I arrived two hours ahead of time. When the bus pulled up, Elvis was the first one off and came running straight to me saying, I knew you d be here waiting for me. Slim Whitman jokingly yelled out, Get away from her, that s my girl. Elvis said, Oh no, you don t!

Elvis said he was hungry and so was I, so we walked about three blocks to a restaurant to pick up some hamburgers and cokes and lemon tarts. We brought them back to the theater and sat backstage talking and eating. Elvis loved those lemon tarts and managed to eat eleven of the twelve we bought and he said I saved this one for you, Jan.

We discussed our families, our school years and our love for God. We both were about the same age and really did have a lot in common. When I told him that one day he d be one of the greatest singers this world would ever know, he very humbly thanked me and said, Jan, with your love and faith, I 11 always get by.

There was an old upright piano in the corner and Elvis went over and started playing some hymns. I remember him playing In The Garden and Whispering Hope. We both enjoyed singing together as he played. Then he turned and looked at me and said, Let s sing Moonlight and Roses . It was when we finished this song that Elvis told me that his favorite rose was the black rose.

We took some pictures and then decided to walk around the block a couple of times. During this time Elvis asked me to be his steady girl.

I was so touched and honored at his request. I ll never forget the feeling that came over me, it was like an angel was there. I told him that from the moment I d met him he seemed like the brother I d never had and I would always love him as such. It was as though he d been a part of me from the beginning.

After a brief disappointing look, he said he understood, but that I must believe that he would always love me as long as he lived and I would always be close to his heart at all times.

It was nearing time for him to get ready for the evening performance, so we went back into the theater and he and I sang Let Me Call You Sweetheart and danced while we sang. We could have danced all night, but we knew the show must go on.

I will never forget that memorable night and when
I m asked to dance now, it brings back memories of
that night with the King.

What many people don t know is that Elvis loved
country music. He did not give himself the name of The
King of rock and roll. The public pinned that on him.

One of the most beautiful country songs ever written
is You Gave Me A Mountain. Elvis sang this song with
meaning from the bottom of his heart. I watched the
tears mount up in his eyes while he sang it.

One time he said, Anne Murray should be called A
Country Music Angel because no voice on earth could
compare to hers.

Elvis could sing any kind of song, be it country, pop,
blues or rock. No one could sing spiritual songs like he
could.I think he proved himself in more ways than one.
He became the world s greatest entertainer with a string
of unending hits.

My life was blessed because of the times I spent with
him and I will always treasure his friendship and love.

FOLLOWING HIS CAREER

In just a few short months, Elvis Presley Fan Clubs began to form all over the nation. Soon his records were selling like hot cakes and Elvis memorabilia was being made right and left.

He sent me one of the first handkerchieves with his picture in the corners. Then there were lipsticks and small record players and key rings, etc. Then came the songbooks, photos, posters, all of which Elvis sent me at different times. I also participated in quite a few of his clubs.

It wasn t long until Uncle Sam called Elvis into the Army and it was my great pleasure to go to Europe on the same ship he did, the U.S. Randall. I knew there was no way that the American people would forget the guy who could sing like no one else. He certainly realized this when his tour of duty ended in Germany and he came back home to all of the fans he left behind.

As time went on, one record after another, then one movie after another, his popularity grew and grew. Fan Clubs began to organize all over the world and I became a part of helping them and started holding Elvis Conventions and Societies. I traveled quite a bit and made sure I d have one of these meetings in every place I stayed for any length of time. My travels took me to Hawaii and to the Orient where the fans loved Elvis so much and longed to see him perform in person.

My daughters, then very young, anticipated the day when they would be able to see their favorite entertainer in person. All of us had been collecting everything we could find on or about Elvis during this time. The record collection had become enormous as well as the photos and clippings.

Finally, in February of 1970, it was announced that
Elvis would be performing at the Rodeo in Houston,
Texas. So you know where mother and daughters were
headed then!

When it came time for Elvis to appear, lights went
out and there were thousands screaming, just the way
they did back in the fifties. Suddenly, he appeared in a
beautiful white jumpsuit and started singing in his own
familiar way and I turned and looked at both my girls
to find tears of joy flowing down their faces because
they were so glad to see him for the first time. Let s face
it, that multitude of people were there for one reason
and that was to see and hear Elvis!

We purchased a few more things to go with our
collection and obtained a membership blank to join
another club.

It was a memorable event and all the way home we
talked about the beautiful songs Elvis sang at the rodeo
which included Release Me and The Wonder Of You
and about the reaction of the fans and how we all
wanted to see him again very soon.

In fact, just three months later we decided to let
Memphis be a part of our summer vacation. The timing
was very good because we were there at Graceland
when Elvis came home. I have many memories of this
visit including some rare photographs that Elvis gave
me for my scrapbook collection.

The Elvis Parties and Conventions continued to grow.
I directed and hosted as many as time would allow,

The following year, 1971, took us to Las Vegas for
his opening there. It was here that he gave a treasured
black scarf to Angie, my youngest daughter and it was
here that enabled me to meet many famous entertainers
and movie stars.

The strength poured forth into each performance in
Las Vegas was astounding. He seemed to out do himself
there more for some reason and people came from all
over the world to see his show.

My family and I were always treated with great
respect in Las Vegas and of course, spent a great deal

of time with all those associated with Elvis. As time passed, Elvis was making personal appearances too numerous to mention all over the United States and Hawaii, too.

1972 brought him back to San Antonio, Texas for the first time since 1956. It was during our annual Fiesta week and I began making preparations for a banquet to be held prior to his show as well as a big Elvis party at my home. My daughters and I were busy making souvenirs to give out to all the guests then they arrived.

We always had a variety of entertainment, fans that would sing Elvis songs and we would supply the back up music since my girls and I played instruments and sang. Delicious buffets were always served and games and prizes galore.

Everyone that ever attended one of my gatherings enjoyed themselves to the fullest extent and always wanted to know when the next one would be.

Showtime finally came and when Elvis entered the stage he was greeted with a welcome like I d never witnessed before. San Antonio was indeed ready to see and hear the guy from Tupelo who had been sweeping the nation with his rendition of Hound Dog and crowding the theatres with his good clean movies. As usual, every seat was taken and he put a that was Long remembered.

Personal appearances were set for other cities in Texas and we found ourselves traveling to Houston and Dallas very soon. Every city brought sold out appearances. When word first spread that Elvis was coming to town people would immediately tie up the phone lines to the radio stations and all the arenas to find out where they could purchase tickets and how soon they could get them.

Some would travel from city to city, days ahead of time and camp out in front of the ticket offices all night just to be sure of getting a ticket.

1974 brought Elvis back to San Antonio, this time he looked better than ever dressed in his Peacock suit. When he entered the stage he posed momentarily for

his fans to take pictures, then on with the show, with
tunes like I Got a Woman and If You Love Me, Let Me
Know. Well, the audience let him know how much they
loved him!

I had seen Elvis do his rendition of You Gave Me A
Mountain many times before but never with such meaningful
effort as he used at this performance. This was a concert
that will long be remembered and it was on this visit
that Elvis left his gold bracelet for one of my daughters.

August 27,1976, was the last appearance that Elvis
gave in San Antonio. Dressed in a beautiful blue suit, he
gave his fans his best in a song that he had made famous,
called Hurt. The highlight of the show was his bicentennial
rendition of America The Beautiful, which even brought
tears to his eyes as well as the listening audience. This
had to be the greatest concert of all time and the love in
my heart multiplied for Elvis, as he expressed his God-
given love and talent to his audience.

Jan Edwards & Elvis Presley

Elvis

Elvis singing Baby Let s Play House
for the first time

JANIS MARTIN - THE FEMALE ELVIS

By the end of 1955, another star joined the Old
Dominion Barn Dance and was well on her way to fame
and fortune. Janis Darlene Martin, known as The
Female Elvis Presley, was born in Sutherlin, Virginia.
Starting at the age of four, being interested in music,
Janis entered every talent contest that came her way
and won first place in all of them.

Jewell Martin, mother of Janis, traveled with her
daughter, promoting her and enjoying all the aspects of
what the music world had to offer. The demand for
performances all over the state of Virginia, the Carolinas
and Ohio was indeed great and each performance
brought another contract for return engagements.

By the time Janis was fifteen, she had made
numerous appearances on the Barn Dance and she had
now decided to make it her home. Her long blonde hair
worn in pony tail style and her beautiful blue eyes,
accented her vivacious stage personality and her
audience waited patiently for her time to perform. You
could hear the whistles from the guys and screams
from all the teenagers.

Janis mastered every song and movement that Elvis
Presley had ever done. He was her idol and she was
determined to follow in his footsteps. Like Elvis, in
many ways the songs kinda got a grip on her and that s
why RCA eventually gave her a contract and tagged her
The Female Elvis Presley.

Her first recording for RCA Victor was a song she
wrote called Drugstore Rock N Roll. It was a sellout

across the country in no time! Next came My Boy
Elvis and this really hit the charts with a bang!

Janis could sing Blue Suede Shoes or Hound Dog
and imitate Elvis to perfection. Every time she finished
the audience would give a thunderous applause which
called for encores. She also sang the country ballads
like Blue Moon Turns To Gold Again.

Even though she was a regular now on the Barn
Dance, soon the demand came for her to tour the
country with Pat Boone and the Hilltoppers and
requests were coming in from overseas to bring her
show over there.

Forming her own Band called E.P. Express, named
after Elvis, Janis began her travels to Holland, Belgium,
France and England. They welcomed her and her music,
as well as her imitation of Elvis because they had wanted
Elvis to perform over there but that never transpired, so
Janis was the next best thing to him. Every where she
appeared in concert, tickets were sold out and return
engagements were booked way ahead of time.

I used to have so much fun backstage at the Barn
Dance helping her get ready for the show. Sometimes
we would go over to the little coffee shop on the corner
and play Elvis records on the little table jukebox.

When Elvis passed away, Janis tried to get away
from performing out of respect for him but she received
letters every day begging her to do appearances, both in
the states and overseas. The demand was so great that
she felt she had to oblige. This was something that was
very hard for her to do because she adored Elvis so
much and to this day, she still has a rose pressed in
her Bible that he gave her when they met at RCA back
in the 50 s. Janis says, Those days will never come
again, it s a memory that I ll cherish forever.

Janis and I kept in close contact through the years
and even in her late fifties she was still making
personal appearances and singing those Elvis songs.

Carl Perkins, better known as Mr. Blue Suede
Shoes, was very dedicated to every show he ever
played. I recall a show that we attended in Texas where

only a small group of people showed up because of severe weather conditions. Carl and some of the other Opry performers went ahead with the show anyway. You can imagine how hard it was to play and sing for so few people.

When the show was over, Carl and I visited and he said the small group didn t bother him at all, that he was more than glad to play for the fans. This is always his happy attitude. He s quick to show how grateful he is for his fan s loyalty.

When you think of Slim Whitman, you remember the beautiful song Indian Love Call. This international star won the hearts of many with his unique voice. When I first met him in Norfolk, Virginia in the 50 s, I found him to be very modest but one who loved to tease. I was fascinated by his left-hand guitar playing.

Hank Snow, the Singing Ranger from Canada, always impressed me with his love for little children. Of all the songs he made famous, Yellow Roses stood out as my very favorite.

Jimmie Rodgers Snow, toured with his father, Hank Snow in the 50 s and he and Elvis used to love looking through the movie and teen magazines in between shows.

I spent quite some time visiting with Skeeter Davis after a show in Virginia in 1955. She had beautiful long curly hair and when she finished the show she put her hair up on top of her head so elegantly and signed autographs for a long period. She told me about suffering a great loss when Betty Jack Davis, her singing partner, passed away in 1953. It was the two of them that made the big hit, I Forgot More Than You ll Ever Know famous. Another friend stepped in to help fill the void. Her name was Georgia.

My mother and Dad both played the harmonica and so did I, so it was a pleasure for me to meet Onie Wheeler, who had a unique style on the harmonica. He had a very popular song called Onie's Bop.

When I met him in Richmond, Virginia in 1955, he was travelling with the Hank Snow Band, and was just gaining popularity. He was a friendly guy and spent quite some time with me talking about his admiration for Wayne Raney, another well known harmonica player.

Carl Smith, sometimes called Mr. Personality, was a tall and handsome guy that all the girls flocked to see whenever he came to town. He looked sharp in his western suits. Let Old Mother Nature Have Her Way, started the ball rolling for him and he became one of the nation's biggest country performers. One time married to June Carter, they had a daughter named Carlene, who is also in the music business.

I met Ferlin Husky shortly after his hit song with Jean Shepard swept the country called, A Dear John Letter. The talents this man has far surpasses many performers. His great showmanship on stage, coupled with his comic presentation of Simon Crum, kept his audience wondering what he was going to do next. He could imitate all of the entertainers, including Kitty Wells. We used to say he sounded more like them than they did themselves. Kitty Wells and Red Foley had a record out called One By One that they sang together and Ferlin cracked the audience up when he impersonated this one. In a matter of seconds, he could go into a beautiful song like Gone or On The Wings Of A Dove. He was every bit a gentleman and so appreciative of his fans.

Abbie Neal, a long time veteran in show business, was once a disc jockey on WAMO in Pittsburgh. She also had an all girl band known as the Ranch Girls and they performed on the Wheeling Jamboree. When they left Wheeling they joined the Barn Dance in Richmond and became favorites of many Barn Dance goers.

When I first met Abbie in the early 50 s, I knew we would have a lasting friendship. She was a beautiful lady and she loved to sit and talk with me about her accomplishments and she was happiest when she was playing Orange Blossom Special on her fiddle. We often remarked that she turned the fiddle every way but loose. She was also an excellent guitarist as she mastered Steel Guitar Rag and she always got standing ovations. Abbie always wore colorful cowgirl suits with a western hat.

In 1983, she was awarded a star in the Sidewalk Of Fame in front of the Capitol Theater Building in Wheeling. Her travels took her and her Band across the country and overseas where they played to packed houses. In later years Abbie moved to Reno, Nevada and began doing volunteer work with seniors.

Another star from Pennsylvania who joined the Barn Dance in Richmond was yodeling Buddy Allen. He gave his best at Chime Bells and could hold a note longer than anyone I d ever heard. My dad became one of his greatest admirers and we often visited with Buddy after his performance.

Zag, the Ozark Mountain Boy, was one of the top attractions on the Barn Dance. Always smiling and blushing while singing, he bounced all around the stage while doing one of Tommy Collins hits called, You d Better Not Do That. Zag and I were always feeding each other donuts, one of our favorite foods.

Jewel Martin, Jan & Janis

Janis & Jan at WRVA Studios

Ferlin Husky
& Jan

Carl Perkins &
Terrie
Edwards
(Jan s daughter)

Skeeter Davis
& Georgia

The Davis
Sisters with Jan

Jimmie Rodgers Snow & Jan

Hank Snow & Terrie

MRS. JIMMIE RODGERS

In January of 1956, we moved to Lawton, Oklahoma. I cannot begin to explain how sad I was to leave all my friends at the Barn Dance but I vowed to return come vacation time. Before I left, they all went together and gave me nice gifts. We only lived in Oklahoma three months when we found out we were moving to San Antonio, Texas.

When we arrived, it didn t take me long to find out that the Barn Dance aired each Saturday over the CBS Network. I figured I could cope with anything as long as I could hear that. Every Saturday Sunshine Sue would dedicate a song to me and the Fan Club and we talked several times by phone.

Summertime rolled around before I knew it and we were on our way back to Virginia to see our friends and to bring my mother back to Texas with us since my father had passed away.

We spent two Saturdays at the Barn Dance and on one of those Sue was given an award for her outstanding contribution to music. I was pleased to be a part of the celebration. A lot of the Barn Dance members had gone on to join the Opry in Nashville and new faces graced the stage.

In February of 1957, our first child was born, a little girl whom we named Terrie Sue, after my wonderful friend, Sunshine Sue. Sue was so honored by her namesake and she sent gifts for our baby right away.

When Terrie Sue was four months old, we took our vacation and headed back to Virginia again to spend time with Sue and all our friends. The first Sunday we were there, Sue and John had a big outdoor picnic at their home in Medley Grove, just outside of Richmond, for us. Friends were invited and we had a marvelous time.

Sue prepared all the food herself and she baked a table full of different kinds of pies. When I asked her why she made so many she said, I wanted to make a variety just for you all. She was the best cook and could make the best homemade bread I ever tasted. I had some of her bread many times before when she d bring it to the theater. We had all kinds of sodas and iced tea and watermelon. What a wonderful feast!

Sue had a hammock that she put Terrie Sue in while we were eating and as soon as we finished she picked Terrie Sue up and held her the rest of the evening. We went inside and sat around talking and looking through photograph albums for a long time.

I always hated to leave because Sue made us feel so much at home and when it was time to go she sent us off with breads and pies.

In 1957, Sunshine Sue retired from the Barn Dance due to ill health but she went back for a final curtain call in 1975 due to the demands of her loyal fans. Most of the original cast was there to join the soft voiced lady as she brought once again a standing ovation and housewide sing-along of You Are My Sunshine. Sadly, it wasn t long after this appearance that my dear friend and ray of sunshine passed away, leaving memories that will always be treasured.

It was in November of 1957 that I first met another gracious and elegant woman by the name of Carrie Rodgers that lived very near me in San Antonio. We had spoken over the telephone earlier that afternoon. She was so dear and graciously insisted that I go and pay her a visit that very evening. Having always been associated with country music and admiring the songs of her late husband, America s Blue Yodeler, it was indeed a pleasure to be going to her home.

My knock on at the door that evening brought this response, Hello, come in darling and give me that precious baby, referring to our little Terrie Sue, who was then nine months old. Holding her close and planting a kiss on her cheek, Mrs. Rodgers remarked how it brought back memories of her daughter, Anita, when she was a baby.

After we sat down in a room filled with reminders of her husband s career, she gave us some large thick albums to look through while she went into the kitchen to gather all the goodies she d prepared for us and a fresh pot of coffee. Coming back into the living room, she reminded me how happy she was to have us over for a little light buffet because most of her meals were eaten in restaurants since she lived alone.

In between snacks and sips of coffee, I saw many photographs of the Rodgers family, some dating back to April of 1920, when she and Jimmie were married in Meridian, Mississippi.

Photos of her mother and father were displayed proudly. She spoke with great pride about being the daughter of a minister and about the love their family possessed and shared with all whom they met.

Throughout the evening, she frequently spoke of the love that bound her and Jimmy together and of the long, lonely hours spent after his passing. She never ceased being grateful for his phonograph records to listen to and she made it a point to listen to them especially when she was feeling blue. She constantly followed Jimmie on his road tours and filled scrapbooks with every clipping she could find from every newspaper in any city they went.

Since she and I both played the piano, she suggested that we play some of her husband s best loved songs. We played and sang Soldier s Sweetheart and Waiting For A Train.

Her profound gratitude to Ernest Tubb was discussed, in that he d been such a help to her in time of need and she proudly showed me the television he bought her.

Shortly before Jimmie Rodgers passed away, he asked Carrie to write a book about his life and this she did with much love and inspiration. She presented me

with an autographed copy and I still find myself
glancing through its pages very often.

This dear lady and I became close friends. We often
shared lunch in quiet restaurants around town and she
always requested that I bring my little Terrie Sue for
her to hold. When Terrie Sue became one years old, it
was Mrs. Rodgers that gave her a birthday party and
showered her with gifts.

This beautiful lady loved good music and had
compassion for all mankind. If I may borrow the words
from Jimmie, Carrie Rodgers was everything that was
sweet, true and fine.

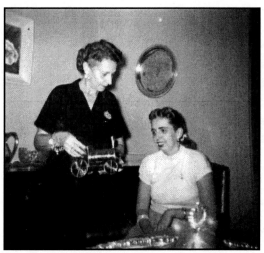

Mrs. Rodgers showing Jan some things given
to her by her husband

Carrie Rodgers

Mrs. Jimmie Rodgers & Terrie Sue

Mrs. Rodgers & Jan

Mrs. Rodgers & Jan sharing a cup of tea

Mrs. Rodgers with a photo of daughter Anita on the wall

VISITING WITH A VARIETY OF STARS

The last part of 1958, I sailed to Europe on the same ship that Elvis was on, called the U.S.S. Randall. I spent three years in France and continued my correspondence with my country music friends. The country songs were very popular all over Europe and many of the entertainers went overseas on USO Tours. Tex Ritter was well known and often visited France and Germany.

Our second little girl, Angie, was born in France in 1960. I ve always thought she was a born musician, because as soon as she learned to walk she d go over to the radio and start dancing to the music.

In 1961, we were back stateside living in El Paso, Texas. Many Grand Ole Opry shows came to this city and was sponsored by KHEY. It was here that I met Johnny Cash. His record of Johnny Yuma was a big hit at the time and was played constantly on the radio. On the same show were the Carter Sisters and Mother Maybelle. It was indeed a pleasure to talk with them again after such a long time. It seemed like old times back at the Barn Dance.

From time to time several entertainers appeared like the Wilburn Brothers and Loretta Lynn, George Morgan, Mac Wiseman and Marty Robbins. It was always fun to watch Loretta do her dance on stage, a good old hoedown.

When Patsy Cline came to town, every seat in the auditorium was taken. She indeed had a special voice, one that is still popular today.

In 1964, I returned to San Antonio. This beautiful city was such a part of me now, they say once a Texan, always a Texan. One thing for sure, we had good country music shows here at the Municipal Auditorium, more often than any place I d ever been and we had great disc jockey s to introduce the entertainers. Guys like Jim Travis and Max Gardner. They were always on top of all the latest records.

The summer of 64 found me in Nashville at the Grand Ole Opry. There was no feeling like being at the Ryman Auditorium. They sold fans outside the door for twenty-five cents and everyone bought them to keep cool while watching the show. I had visited with many of the performers the night before at the Friday night Opry over at WSM. Countless pictures were taken and many of the stars spent time with my two little girls. Del Wood just loved my girls and wanted to keep them with her.

I talked with Doyle Wilburn and his wife and cute little girl. She looked just like a little doll. We also talked to String Bean for a long time. He was a person everyone enjoyed being around.

In 1968 I left for Japan. I found country music to really be booming over there. The Japanese were experts at mastering the songs made famous by American performers.

I met an all-girl western band called, Western Angels who had performed all over the Orient at Military clubs.

We became good friends and I taught them all of the latest country songs in English and my daughters and I traveled all over Japan with them. Nobuko was the leader of the band and came to live with us while we were there and also came back to the states with us for three years.

I was her personal manager and Billy Deaton, who had his office here at the time, was her booking agent. She was a fine musician. She played the lead electric guitar and sang country ballads all in English. Her cowgirl suits were all handmade and sometime she would wear her kimono with accessories for special

parties that she pLayed for. She was fortunate to
appear on the Grand Ole Opry, thanks to Billy Deaton.

My first meeting with Roy Clark was at our Hemisfair
in 1968. I ve never met anyone who enjoyed life more
than Roy. He saw everything through a healthy laugh
and found some humor even in the worst situations.

Roy Orbison had a style all his own and when he
came to San Antonio the people couldn t get enough of
his beautiful voice, especially when he sang Crying. It
always called for encores. He was a very nice guy but
kinda shy.

One of my favorite songs has always been Truck
Driving Man and George Hamilton IV had a big hit
with this song.

Pee Wee King, one of the dearest people I knew in
country music, sent me snapshots of him and his band
back in the late forties and early fifties. When Pee Wee
and Redd Stewart wrote Tennessee Waltz they wrote a
masterpiece.

Hank Thompson and the Brazos Valley Boys played
at the Golden Stallion here in San Antonio in the late
70 s. He made you feel good to be around him and he
enjoyed taking pictures.

Jerry Lee Lewis is one heck of a survivor. He can
sing any kind of song and rip a piano apart. We had
many good conversations when he played at Randy s
Rodeo in San Antonio. He always sang my favorite song
for me called To Make Love Sweeter For You.

John Conlee really packed the Longhorn Ballroom in
Dallas. Rose colored glasses were all over the place in
honor of his song by that title.

In 1977, I had the pleasure of meeting one of the
nicest and most talented musicians that ever performed
on stage. David Proud, born in Canada, who now makes
his home in Reno, Nevada, plays the Nevada Circuit. He
is absolutely astounding to watch and hear. I met him
while he was on a cross-country tour that brought him
to San Antonio to entertain at the Swiss Chalet.
Besides singing in his own style, he can imitate to
perfection all other performers, such as Elvis, Tom

Jones, Marty Robbins and Satchmo. To say that his tribute to America, his own special rendition of American Trilogy, is super fantastic, is stating it mildly. When you watch him do this, it touches your heartstrings and brings more than one encore and always a standing ovation.

It was an honor to be in the audience watching the Oak Ridge Boys back in the 70 s when they first started their career in country music. San Antonio s Turtle Creek Country Club was one of their first stops and they packed the place from wall to wall. I don t know which was the best, watching Joe bounce around all over the stage while singing or listening to those deep bass chords that Richard sent out, but I knew they d be a number one act before too long. I had a wonderful time backstage with them. I had known Richard from when he was traveling with Elvis. These guys are all down to earth people and are always helping someone. Their hits have been unending and their most requested is Elvira.

Everyone remembers a classic called Almost Persuaded sung by the one and only David Houston.

They don t come any nicer than Mel Tillis. Mel came to a little town just outside of San Antonio called Universal City and signed autographs for fans before appearing at a local club that evening. I ll never forget when I walked into the record shop where he was visiting with the fans, he caught a glimpse of me and yelled clear across the store, Come on over here, baby. It was such fun to visit with him. He s one of the most loved entertainers in the music field. Always kidded about his stuttering, it has never affected his proven talent in songs like Let s Chase Each Other Round The Room Tonight.

Marvin Rainwater spent a short time as on the Old Dominion Barn Dance and was such a likeable fellow and sang that happy go lucky song, Gonna Find Me A Bluebird. Both he and Shirley Hunter were new, starting their careers back in the 50 s.

A duet team from Tennessee came Southwest in the
early 70 s, stopping in San Antonio to do personal
appearances and spent time with me at my home.
Jamie and Buddy sang all of the top country songs.
They especially liked Ray Price and Merle Haggard.
They both used red white and blue guitars and dressed
western style.

J.D. Sumner will always be remembered for the great
contribution he and the Stamps Quartet gave to the Elvis
Presley shows. With his deep bass voice, he was just
right for those special songs that Elvis sang in a spiritual
moment of triumph. Elvis and J.D. were very close
friends and J.D. had so many good memories of their
travels together and never failed to call Elvis the best. I
had many occasions to talk with J.D. through the years
and he is most sincere person.

The duo of Beverly and Marcia are well known
around Connecticut. Beverly Chariott used to be with
Abbie Neal and the Ranch Girls in the 60 s. This is
when I first met Bev and she was undoubtedly the best
accordionist I d ever heard. When she played The
Yellow Rose Of Texas Polka everyone stood up and
took notice. We had the good fortune of meeting in
Japan while I was there and Bev and Abbie Neal and
the Ranch Girls spent some time with me in my home.
They had an extended tour in the Far East playing at
all the military bases.

When Riders In The Sky announced they were going
to appear at a local school in San Antonio, I knew I had
to attend their show. I have always loved traditional
cowboy songs and these guys are the nearest thing to
the Sons Of The Pioneers who brought us all the tunes
from the west.

Ranger Doug has a beautiful voice and does a fine
job of yodeling. I ve never yet figured out how he can
hold those notes so long.

Woody Paul is one of the best fiddlers in the
business and he does so many good rope tricks during
their performances.

Too Slim can keep you laughing the whole time with his jokes and cowboy humor. They always insist on doing things the cowboy way.

There were so many children present at this school and it did my heart good to see how they enjoyed good clean fun as much as I.

It was indeed a pleasure to meet the guys and talk with them. They were all very friendly and took time to visit with everyone after their show.

How can anyone possibly say enough about dear Minnie Pearl and dear Roy Acuff, the foundations of country music? The Grand Ole Opry will always exist here and hereafter as long as there s such a thing as memory. Minnie brought so much happiness through her humor. When I met her in the 60 s, she gave me the biggest hug and had such a beautiful smile. I loved it when she would sing Careless Love.

I remember buying the old 78 s by Roy Acuff. I loved to hear him sing Put My Little Shoes Away. He always welcomed every performer with enthusiasm and wished the best for all of them. I had the golden opportunity of meeting Mr. Roy back in the late 50 s and I will never forget his friendly manner.

The early 80 s recognized a new Texas Band called Spur Of The Moment. San Antonio based, they played regularly at the top country western clubs, military bases and traveled to other cities as well.

Terrie and Angie Edwards organized the group. Terrie played bass, sang solos and wrote some of her own songs. A faithful admirer of the Judds, she sang many of their hits.

Angie, a lead guitar picking wizard, started playing the instrument at an early age and can compete with the best of them, even playing the guitar behind her head.

Terry Powell could bring the house down with his rendition of The Auctioneer, a song that just anyone could not do. He also mastered a lot of Ray Price songs.

Mike Griffith did a great job of playing San Antonio Rose on the trumpet and got many requests for a song he sang called Miles and Miles Of Texas.

From time to time Spur Of The Moment hired
different ones to play in their band and I even sung
with them at the VFW Club dances.

Terrie and Angie, of course, are my daughters and
I m extremely proud of them and their talents. They ve
recorded a couple of records, songs that Terrie wrote.
Mike Houston also played with the Band and he
sang a lot of Merle Haggard songs. A very talented
musician, with a strong clear voice. He s also recorded
a couple of songs which he wrote.

You don t come across many female lead guitarists
and Angie is extraordinary. She has a trademark song
that she picks the fire out of called, Guitar Boogie
Shuffle. She makes it look so easy for the rest of us
and she enjoys every moment she s playing.

J.C. Herrera was a fantastic drummer and played
with Spur of the Moment for quite a while. He always
got a lot of requests to do Guitars and Cadillacs.

There s a great Band in El Paso by the name of Stray
Bullet. They keep up with all the top country tunes.

What a wonderful friend Red River Dave McEnery
was. We spent a lot of time talking about the good old
days when so many of the performers were starting
their careers.

Dave was born in San Antonio, not too far from the
Alamo. By the time he was eighteen, he was singing,
writing songs and performing rope tricks and had his
own radio show in 1932. Six years later he had become
America s singing cowboy thanks to WOR in New York.
He also sang on a radio station in my hometown in
Petersburg, Virginia in the 30 s.

Dave wrote and recorded his own songs and they
were all about what s happening in the world. Recently
he wrote The Soldier s Letter (Desert Shield Song)
which explained his feelings about the war in the
Persian Gulf. It became very popular. He also wrote
Amelia Earhart s Last Flight which was very popular
years ago.

After spending several years in California at Knott s
Berry Farm, he returned to San Antonio where he

continued to write and became a cowboy evangelist and also sang on a local station here singing gospel songs.

We often talk about his good friend Texas Jim Robertson. Texas Jim was one of my very favorite singers back in the early 40 s and I loved his record of Filipino Baby. Jim and Dave traveled all up and down the east coast early in their careers searching for places to play and sing.

To know Red River Dave is to love him. He s been around for over 70 years and had been in the company of stars at one time or another and often shared some of his golden memories with me.

Conway Twitty has had more hits than anyone and his audience loves that growl in his voice, especially the ladies. My own personal favorite by him is Hello Darlin. It s a song that no one else could attempt to try, it was made for Conway.

He recently said so long to his drummer partner, Pork Chop, who had been with him, fronting his shows, always introducing Conway, for over 30 years.

Conway has always given extra time in his shows. He stayed on stage till the crowd had heard almost every song he d ever done. I watched him do a two hour show once in Beaumont, Texas in the summer when the temperature was way over a hundred degrees and the air conditioning went out in the auditorium where he was performing. We were all so hot and miserable and Conway was about to fall over from the heat, but he kept right on until he finished the show. He was a real trooper.

Gary Morris has one of the most beautiful voices I ve ever heard. He holds your full attention when he sings Wind Beneath My Wings. A more modest and humble person you ll never meet than Gary.

Alabama has certainly had a string of hits since they ve been in the music business. They are so loved and they have done so many good things for their home state of Alabama. I think it s wonderful that three people that are kin to each other, decided to stick together in country music. Randy, Jeff and Teddy are cousins. Also, Mark is an excellent drummer and they give us great songs like Mountain Music.

Kenny Rogers, he s the best! I remember being so crazy about him even when he had The First Edition. I started collecting everything I could find on him way back then. Kenny has a style all his own and you just fall in love with everything he sings. When he came to Sea World in San Antonio there wasn t room for one more person to crowd in, believe me, and we all went crazy when he did The Gambler.

Where would we be without the great Disc Jockeys that play all the beautiful country and western songs each day and evening on the good old radio?

Scoopie Bruce Harper kept the turntables busy in Tennessee for over four decades, playing the records his audience wanted to hear. A veteran of World War II, Bruce was drafted in 1941 and spent four years in the Army Air Corps. He was engaged in a fighter group in the Panama Canal Zone and in England on B17 s Flying Fortresses, which flew over 350 combat missions.

Receiving an honorable discharge in 1945, the desire came a few years later to attend Broadcasting School. Upon graduation, Bruce set out to do what he loved best, spin records by performers that later became his close personal friends. He was the first country music DJ to work full-time in Tennessee. Some of his radio station credits include, WAMG in Gallatin, WMTS in Murfressboro and WENO in Madison. His popularity soared when he joined WLAC in Nashville.

He earned the nickname Scoopie one day when he was told to go and scoop up some news. Before long his listeners were addressing his letters to Scoopie Bruce Harper.

In 1968, Bruce was awarded the Gold Microphone, by the Radio Announcing News.

Scoopie told me that he remembers when radio sold everything from baby chicks and rose bushes to Hank Williams songbooks.

His knowledge of country music is extraordinary and his love and devotion for the Grand Ole Opry and all its

performers is unending. His heart holds many loving
memories of Grant Turner, his dear close friend for
years and he said the good times with Webb Pierce and
Marty Robbins can never be replaced. He spoke of Eddy
Arnold, as one of the best in the business.

In his spare time he would emcee shows and do PR
work for R.O.P.E. (Reunion Of Professional Entertainers)
of which he was a lifetime member and he served with
the American Legion Post 82, in Nashville. He also does
some part-time work as a DJ.

He told me that Nashville is the friendliest place in
the country and that he never called his work a daily
routine because he loved anything that had to do with
country music. He s been in several movies and
recorded two songs early in his career.

When I asked this tall man with the white suit,
purple tie and shirt and the big cowboy hat what it was
that made the best DJ, his reply was simple and to the
point. He said, Just be familiar with all the songs both
old and new and claim the artists and the writers as
your friends.

Scoopie kept in touch with me twice a week and he
always called me his San Antonio Rose. What a kind
man and what a dedication to country music.

The tall rugged looking sort of a guy, who had
number one hits every year in the 60 s was one of my
favorites. Buck Owens could sing Together Again like
no other and the fine entertainment he projected during
the show Hee Haw was a family welcome in homes
across the nation.

I met him overseas at one of the military bases where
he and his band were playing and then later he came to
San Antonio and I got to visit with him and Don Rich.

I liked the fact that Buck never got in a hurry about
anything. He took things as they came and enjoyed life.
He was very kind and friendly to all his fans. It was
very sad to see him give up his career not long ago, but
it was nice to see him perform his last concert in Texas.

Charley Pride stepped into the music field in the 60 s
and brought us some of those great songs that Hank

Williams blessed us with. Charley did them so well and
was constantly asked to sing Kawliga. I met Charley
when he came to Randy s Rodeo in San Antonio and
then again in Las Vegas, Nevada when I was visiting
Elvis. He was full of gratitude for his climb to success
in country music.

Dave Rowland is that handsome little guy with a
mighty voice that teams up with those two gorgeous
girls called Sugar. You can bet when Dave s in town
that the gals flock to see him after the show. Some of
us used to call him the Ben Casey of country music.
We just thought he looked like a compassionate, good
looking doctor.

My daughters sure had a good time talking with T.
Graham Brown, in Nashville. He loves colorful jackets
and commented how he liked Terrie s.

Ricky Skaggs is a multi-talented musician and gives
us that traditional bluegrass music like Bill Monroe. I
admire Ricky s spiritual feelings. He s a great guy and
gives us some songs that touch the soul.

When Jeanne Pruett s dynamic song Satin Sheets
topped the charts in 1973, someone sent me a set of
purple sheets and pillow cases made of satin. I felt like
a Queen visiting the Waldorf Astoria. Jeanne is a very
classy lady. She s beautiful and friendly and can cook
up a storm. I think often of all the fun times she spent
on *Nashville Now* with Ralph Emery trying to teach him
how to cook and the hilarious way they went about it.
It would be hard for anyone to pass up an opportunity
to go to Jeanne s restaurant at Opryland. The smell of
the good down home country cooking would entice you
inside for the treat of your life.

Another lady who has made hundreds of recipes
available to us through her Country Kitchen Show, is
lovely Florence Henderson. It s such fun to see all the
country music stars visit her show and prepare their
own personal recipes and share them with the fans.

There s one thing for sure! San Antonio is very proud
of George Strait! Why shouldn t they be, when he s got
that certain charisma that draws people to him like a

magnet. George sings those hits with a smile in his voice
and a teased look in his eye, especially when he does
All My Ex s Live In Texas. It s always good to see him
as a participant in San Antonio s Livestock and Rodeo.

When it comes to singing a good song, hosting an
awards show or acting in a serious film Reba McEntire
tops the list. This lady has a winning personality and a
can do attitude that enables her to accomplish
whatever she sets out to do

When all is said and done, the best country music
program to ever hit the air waves was *Nashville Now*,
hosted by Ralph Emery and was indeed, the show of
shows, one that I watched from its beginning. Ralph
has been a major influence in so many of the performer s
careers and yet when he s given credit by them he
immediately turns the gratitude toward the entertainer.

I stood by and watched his actions at a book signing
for his wonderful contribution of Memories. People
were lined up all around the room. When he made his
entrance there was a certain loving feeling that you
couldn t help but have. It was a special moment, one
that you knew you d remember for a long time, I
watched him talk to each individual as though he d
known them all their lives, with that caring,
understanding manner that he so often portrayed on
his show. Some people had five or six books for him to
sign and he patiently signed them personally to each
person with handwriting never tiring.

He s simply a person that you can t be around
without feeling that special kind of love that he projects
and you find yourself wanting to thank him for all he
continues to do to bring country music into our homes
each day.

Nearby, glancing through the pages of a book was Joy,
who is Ralph s wife. A charming and beautiful woman
who supports her husband in all his endeavors and told
me that whatever makes him happy that s her desire.

Ralph Emery is indeed a household word. For
wherever you go, you hear people talking about what a
great show that *Nashville Now* was and about all the

wonderful guests he had on there each night. It makes
one wonder how we ever got along without it!

I m always glad to turn the television on, even now,
to see Doug Kershaw give the old fiddle a workout from
one end of the stage to the other while playing Diggy
Liggy Lo. He s been doing just this since he and his
brother Rusty teamed up in the 50 s. They came to
Virginia and put on a show that you couldn t forget for
a long time. I still remember talking to Doug and
looking up into those big bright eyes that did his
talking for him. I really don t know how he keeps from
ripping his pants while he does all those movements as
he s performing. Between him, Jimmy C. Newman and
Eddie Raven, I knew I had to go to Louisiana and get
some of that good old cajun food they talked about and
folks, you haven t lived until you ve tried dirty rice and
Jambalaya cooked cajun style!

The lady, Dottie West, who brought us so much
sunshine in country music will always be remembered
for her beautiful singing voice and for her willingness to
help others in show business. Dottie enjoyed every
moment of her singing career and she was always ready
to stop and talk with friends and fans.

There s no better way to spend an evening than
listening to the soothing sounds of Floyd Cramer at the
piano. His unique style of playing leaves a lasting
impression among fans all over the world. He s played
on countless records by other artists, including Elvis s
 Heartbreak Hotel. My love for the piano, has certainly
drawn the magic touch of Floyd Cramer to my favorite
list of entertainers. We both play by ear, Floyd starting
at age 5 and me at age 4. It s hard to single out a
favorite Cramer song but Last Date would come close.

Every time I watch Alan Jackson perform, the look in
his eyes, the songs he sings, I m reminded of the days
when Hank Williams touched our hearts. There s a
great connection there. Alan comes nearer to that time
than any other artist. There s just something that
brings Hank to mind, especially when he sings

Midnight In Montgomery. Hank Williams would be proud of Alan Jackson!

Doug Stone s songs tell it like it is. Each one relates to his personal experiences and we can all identify to the same. He has that sincere approach when he s on stage and you feel the emotion he s going through. Warning Labels makes us aware of the do s and don'ts of life.

Shotgun Red is as cute as a bugs ear and brings us so many laughs. Miss Daisy must be very proud of him. It s amazing how he s become such a close part of our family.

Country music fans who love roses have to love the Rose Lady. Lynn Anderson, first appeared on the Lawrence Welk show in the 60 s. Then in 1971, she had her famous song Rose Garden that swept the country. She s a beautiful cowgirl and she always sings and talks with a smile.

Who would have ever guessed that one coin could bring so much response by way of song. Travis Tritt s Here s A Quarter has tied up the phone lines since it became a hit.

Award winning Vince Gill, is a sentimental sort of guy. who pleases his thousands of fans each time he sings When I Call Your Name.

When I first saw Tanya Tucker, she was performing at Astroworld, in Houston, Texas in 1976. She admired Elvis a lot and she opened her show with Burning Love. It was dynamite. Of course, Delta Dawn brought a thunderous applause. Tanya has a fantastic stage personality, especially when she dances to the San Antonio Stroll.

Bobby Bare is our great big teddy bear since he has his own Bear Trap Store, displaying and selling every kind of imaginable. Bobby s just a plain, down to earth guy, always the same whether he s performing in Nashville or 500 Miles Away From Home.

I credit a truck driver in a big old eighteen wheeler with saving my life one time, so I m reminded of this incident each time I hear Kathy Mattea sing Eighteen

Wheels and A Dozen Roses. What a beautiful voice she has!

I met Barbara Mandrell overseas and again in Dallas. Both times she had her entire family with her and they really put on a great show. This was back in the 70 s. Anything and everything that s good, can describe Barbara. She s a lovely lady; talented in so many things, has the deepest respect from her fellow workers and she was country when country wasn t cool.

John anderson really rocked the Rodeo grounds in San Antonio in the 80 s when he sang his big hit Swingin. He s a nice guy and says his fans mean more to him than anything. It s good to see him topping the charts again.

Classy lady, K.T. Oslin sings and writes about the now happenings in today s women s lives. Her record 80 s Ladies was a smash hit. This talented lady is no stranger to Broadway plays and musicals or television. She makes friends wherever she goes and she spends a lot of time talking with her fans. She has that aggressive approach but also that understanding compassion for others. Her touch of Hollywood type charm draws her fans close to her every place she goes.

Mickey Gilley has taught us all that The Girls All Get Prettier At Closing Time. He s one of the nicest guys you d ever want to meet and talk with. He tries to please his fans in every way possible.

There s nothing better than a good story and Tom T. Hall is just the man to give us one. He s centered his songs around everyday stories like Old Dogs and Children and Watermelon Wine.

If you re needing a good laugh, look no further than Mike Snider. Just to listen to him talk in that southern drawl will crack you up. He can really play that banjo though and he s going to make sure you get the address to order his music!

Marty Stuart is a fellow that enjoys every moment in Country Music. He takes things as they come and believes them to be meant that way. Besides being a great singer he leaves all the girls wanting to run their

fingers through that nice head of beautiful hair. When
Marty and Travis Tritt team up together, look out!
You re in for a lot of surprises and some songs that will
tear at your heartstrings.
That tall fellow with the slicked back hair, that
dresses Johnny Cash style and gives a few moves like
him too, is Mark Collie. I especially enjoy his great
album, Born and Raised In Black and White.
Everyone is saying that Michelle Wright is Hollywood
material. She has a lovely voice and the manner in
which she presents herself on stage is totally Vegas
style. Her recording of Take It Like A Man, has soared
her to the top of female performers.
There s nothing like good, clean, comedy and the
man who gave us that was Jerry Clower. He was loved
by so many and appreciated for making us laugh even
on our bluest days.
Two native Texans by the last names of Walker, play
an important part on the Grand Ole Opry. Billy, is that
likeable guy that knows exactly how it feels to be in
Charlie s Shoes and Charlie who says to everybody,
Pick Me Up On Your Way Down.
I remember Lorrie Morgan performing at the Opry
at a very early age and her Dad, George Morgan,
would be mighty proud of her today. She s a woman of
beauty and strength, especially when she wears
Something In Red.
Everything Is Beautiful, says Ray Stevens and he
really believes that. You wouldn t think he d have such
a wonderful singing voice after listening to his comedy.
Many people claim that his is the best show they ve
ever seen. He s also known to be one of the friendliest
guys to visit with.
That cute little gal that you see dancing around the
stage while she s singing Down At The Twist and
Shout, is Mary Chapin Carpenter.
Mel Tillis couldn t be more proud of his daughter,
Pam, as she sky rockets to the top with her number
one hit, Don t Tell Me What To Do. This song broke
the ice for her and she couldn t be happier.

All of Mark Chesnutt s Old Flames Have New
Names but that doesn t stop him from turning out hit
after hit. He has a big career ahead of him. This
Beaumont Texan really pleased his audience at Fiesta
Texas in San Antonio.

Marie Osmond comes from a very talented family and
when I met them all in San Antonio in the 70 s, I found
them to be some of the nicest people I ever talked to. I
remember showing Olive Osmond (Marie s mother) a
little book I d gotten from Mexico when I was there that
had the Osmond s pictures in it and she was so
surprised to see it all written in Spanish. I still have
cards that they sent me after they left Texas, with little
written messages from each of them. It s so good to
know that Marie decided to go the country music route
and she couldn t have chosen a more beautiful song
than Paper Roses to send her to the top of the ladder.
She s such a warm and friendly person and spends her
extra time sponsoring The Children s Miracle Telethon.

Bless Your Heart Freddie Hart, it s so Easy Loving
you. This man has the softest voice in the business and
is so humble and grateful for his fans.

Mark O Connor will definitely be a fiddler in
history. Never before has anyone made it look so
simple and yet given such beautiful melodies as Mark.
He s played on everybody who is anybody s albums
and has made his unique contribution to the
symphony, as well.

How well I remember all the parties my daughters
and I played for, some of which were for local high
school teachers Terrie would always sing Jeannie C.
Riley s record of Harper Valley P.T.A. and the teachers
loved it. Jeannie came out with this song in 1968 and
in no time it had sold five million copies.

I ll bet everyone remembers when that good looking
Spanish fellow came on the scene singing Pass Me
By and Jealous Heart. Johnny Rodriguez won the
hearts of many singing country ballads both in
English and in Spanish.

When I was in grade school, I was given some money each Saturday by my grandmother to go to the three o clock movie to see a western. I was always glad when it was Roy Rogers. I loved his singing and I still have some of the old 78 s he recorded like No Vacancy and My Heart Went That A Way.

I heard David Allan Coe say one time that if he were left out in the desert all alone, with everything he had taken from him, he could still start all over in life. This determination is what gave him such classic hits as Mona Lisa s Lost Her Smile.

Charlie Daniels is a man who loves his country and he speaks his mind. This tall fellow with fiddle in hand and cowboy hat that tends to hide his eyes, reminds us that The South s Gonna Do It Again.

I look back through the years when Billie Joe Royal was a teen idol and I remember the distinctive sound his voice had and still has today. The first word in the song lets you know who the artist is. Funny How Time Slips Away Billie Joe, but you ve grown more delightful and we re looking forward to some more number one hits.

Never in the history of country music, has the overwhelming impact of talent, love and beauty, engrossed the public as much as The Judd s. Naomi and Wynonna won the hearts of everyone with their expressions of love through songs from the very beginning of their career. Mama He s Crazy started the ball rolling and it never stopped. They won award after award and hit the mountain peak with Love Can Build A Bridge, one of the prettiest songs ever written. Blessings to you Naomi, for paving the way for Wynonna, who is an astounding star now in her own right.

No one loves their country more than Lee Greenwood. He has given us what seems to be the second national anthem, God Bless The U.S.A. To hear and see him perform this song, is to love America with all one s heart and to recognize a talent unending.

Whatever you re looking for in the way of entertainment, you ll find it while watching the Statler Brothers show. Their songs all tell a true life story and

their voices blend together for those beautiful old
hymns we love so well. If you need a laugh, Harold can
surely supply you with that. They couldn t have chosen
two better singers than Janie Fricke and Rex Allen, Jr.
to be a part of their musical family. I don t think I ve
ever heard a more beautiful rendition of Deep Purple
than when I heard Rex sing it one Saturday on the
show. Janie has a style all her own and my very favorite
by her is Always Have, Always Will. I can t begin to
tell the Statlers how much I enjoyed the newsletter they
sent me. What a wonderful bunch of guys.

I love banjo music and I was in awe of John
Hartford. He makes it look so easy and I just loved his
little dance he did while playing songs like his famous,
 Gentle On My Mind.

Clifton Jansky is well known for the smashing hit
song, Amarillo By Morning. He has numerous other
hits to his credit. Switching over to gospel music, he
has won the hearts of many San Antonians as well as
the fans across the nation. A more friendly performer
you will never meet. He enjoys spending time with all
of his admirers.

Is it possible to keep a dry eye when Gene Watson
sings his signature song called Farewell Party? I don t
think so! This song definitely has to go down as one of
the greatest in country music.

Del Reeves, a man of many talents has a fantastic
personality and really enjoys entertaining people.
Besides singing the love ballads, he can imitate almost
everyone in the business. My favorite is his imitation of
Roy Acuff. Del also had a hand in bringing another
rising performer to the surface, by the name of Billy
Ray Cyrus, the Achy Breaky Heart throb. We know
he ll be around a long time, because he s packing in the
crowds all over the country and his movements on
stage excite the whole.

My love for train songs started with listening to my
Dad play them on the harmonica. Box Car Willie could
sure treat us to some good time train whistles and sing
all of the famous train songs.

Randy Travis has one of the best voices I ve ever heard. I like every song he s ever done. If I had to choose a favorite it would be On The Other Hand.

One of my most enjoyable evenings was spent at a Ricky Van Shelton rodeo performance. Here s a guy who sings his heart out and accepts awards with tremendous humility.

Garth Brooks song, Unanswered Prayers, is one of the best. I think Garth s prayers have all been answered with his giant rise to fame. He really packs them in wherever he appears for a concert.

Aaron Tippin, I m with you all the way. There s nothing wrong with the radio! Just turn on your favorite country station and go about your business!

Sean Castillo is originally from California. He s been around for a long time performing rockabilly and country music. He spent several years as one of the top acts at Fiesta Texas in San Antonio. His show would offer many songs in tribute to Elvis Presley. Having had the opportunity of knowing Elvis, he would have been proud to know Sean and see his performances. Sean loved Elvis and he proves it over and over when he does Elvis famous song, Baby, Let s Play House, which he always does for me when I attend his show.

Jan & Sean

Sean giving us that big rockabilly smile

Nobuko & Bill Monroe

Nobuko & Billy Deaton

Del Wood

Marvin Rainwater &
Shirley Hunter

Don Reno & Jan

J.D. Sumner

Japanese Band called The Western Angels

Woody Paul

Too Slim

Ranger Doug

Fantastic Lead Guitarist

Angie Houston

Angie Houston

Terrie Edwards

Spur of The Moment

Stray Bullet

Conway Twitty

Alabama

Gary Morris

Kenny Rogers

Roy Orbison

Roy Orbison & Terrie Edwards

Dave Roland

Angie Houston, T. Graham Brown & Terrie Edwards

Ricky Skaggs

George Strait

Reba

Little Miss Nobuko

Dotty West

Lee Greenwood singing God Bless the U.S.A.

Ralph Emery & Jan

Loretta Lynn, Terrie
& Angie

Ernest Tubb

Hank Williams, Jr.

Terrie, Jan, Hank Thompson & Angie

Jan & David Houston

Jan & Jerry Lee Lewis

Jerry Lee Lewis

Jerry Lee with Terrie & Angie

Mel tillis & Jan

David Proud

Jan & David Proud

The Oak Ridge Boys

Duane, Jan & Richard

Terrie, Joe & Jan

Bouncing Joe & Angie

The Judd s

John Connoly

Scoppie Harper

Jan and Sean

Chris Castillo

Sean Castillo

Sergio and Jan

Bobby Baker

Neal McCoy

Clifton Jansky

Spur of the Moment
Mike, Jackie, Terry, Angie and Terrie Sue

One afternoon I went to my mailbox and while there, I met an elderly man. He noticed that I had my book of Memories by Ralph Emery in my hand. He said, I ve been ill for a long time, but as soon as I am able to go to the book store I want to buy that book because I wouldn t miss Ralph s show for nothing and Crook and Chase, I love them so much. I thought that was some mighty sweet words about country music leaders. A friend and I supplied this gentleman with the book he so desired and needless to say it made his life very happy.

Crook and Chase made their audience smile and all their guests were great.

It all goes back to what my dear grandmother taught me as a child. Country music is good clean entertainment and it will be around forever.

Many people have asked me what I think of the current stars of country music. My answer is the world is full of changes and golden opportunities and there are many bright stars on the horizon. Those that wish to participate in this music deserve a chance and support from all of us who have so loved the heart-felt Lyrics from long ago that warmed our hearts and helped us in our everyday activities.

I have been asked who are my current favorites. That s kind of hard to say, but I would have to start with George Strait, Alan Jackson and Toby Keith. There are many more that I enjoy listening to and as time goes on I will continue to support their talents.

It is my sincere wish that those of you who glance through the pages of this book will remember the ones who have brought us happiness through their melodies and the ones who have paved the way for the newcomers of today.

Acknowledgements

To my dear grandmother who planted the love for country music in my early childhood years.

To my parents who made the way possible for my early contacts with the performers.

To the legendary Eddy Arnold for prompting me to learn and appreciate real country music at its best.

To Sunshine Sue, the sweetest lady of song whom I loved endlessly.

To Jim and Jerrie Steinhardt for all the good times we shared playing our favorite tunes.

To Roland whose smiles of neverending encouragement keeps me pressing on to more and more writings.

To Tom Polzine, Christy, and all the MK Publishing Group for doing such an excellent job with putting my book together.

ABOUT THE AUTHOR

Jan Edwards is originally from Petersburg Virginia. Her accomplishments as a public speaker, author and teacher have carried her all over the world and enabled her to meet many celebrities and entertainers. A devoted love for country music prompted her to share personal moments and photographs with other country music fans. Jan s desire to continue her piano playing though the years she attributes fully to Eddy Arnold, as she mastered every song he ever recorded. At the present time Jan makes her home in San Antonio, Texas where she continues to write about the famous legends of yesterday, the incomparable stars of today and the newcomers of tomorrow.

<u>Notes</u>

Notes

Notes

Notes

Notes

Notes